ISBN 978-0-266-86199-7
PIBN 10900920

THE STUDY OF

Music As A Liberal Art

BY

GEORGE SHERMAN DICKINSON

Professor of Music, Vassar College

VASSAR COLLEGE

POUGHKEEPSIE • NEW YORK

1953

THE STUDY OF

Music As A Liberal Art

BY

GEORGE SHERMAN DICKINSON

Professor of Music, Vassar College

VASSAR COLLEGE

POUGHKEEPSIE • NEW YORK

1953

PUBLISHED FROM THE
MARY CONOVER MELLON FUND
FOR MUSIC LITERATURE

THE STUDY OF MUSIC AS A LIBERAL ART

N amount of education in music has always gone with nominal effectiveness on the basis of the *ez faire* individualism of teacher and course. Its ver, has obviously fluctuated with the personali-, and the accumulation of educational benefits eterminate. At times, it is true, such independent often desirable in themselves, have fallen into a ome integrity. But the line of least resistance n the direction of consolidating and perfecting and there are inviting rationalizations which have epreciate the value of the purposefully focussed

ong the liberal arts has thus not practiced the *aissez faire* to any consistent advantage, nor has ially sensitive to movements in the direction of curriculum. It has rather remained substantially e inherited formulae of an orthodox curriculum—inflections of them; or, in revolt, it has ventured ents under the banner of "progressive educa-, though perhaps convincing in their own terms, ny rate do not appear to be especially consonant c liberal arts viewpoint.

valid it may seem to be to lead music education the paths of individualistic endeavor, or to con-ity through continual mild revisions of a conven-lum, or to venture to transplant a "progressive" e level of higher education, the present para-of music education in the colleges is such as to tempt to rethink its problems in other terms. In y will be terms indicated by the general liberal ly, and terms which point to the value of a whole e than a fortuitous or conventional or pragmatic parts.

imple the viewpoint which characterizes an edu-ss readily does that education submit to categorical formulation; on the other hand, the more responsive may it become to embodiment in a general philosophy, which idealizes rather than methodizes, which beckons rather than commands. It is accordingly the first purpose of this essay to try to present a theory of higher education for music as one of the humanities, and in so doing to mark off the particular genius of such education from other possible attitudes.

I. *A Theory of Liberal Music Education*

The distinguishing mark of the liberal education in the arts is its intent to cultivate the aesthetic experience – in music that unique form of artistic response induced by patterns of tone and time.

The most immediate and elemental experience of music accepts the intuition as guide and arbiter. One is more "musical" or less so. It is, no doubt, the prerogative of art to flatter the gift of temperament. Yet the raw intuition alone – except in instances on the threshold of genius – is an unreliable and deceptive agent in the interpretation of the aesthetic experience by the subject of that experience. The mere self-exercise of the intuitive faculty as its own authority is centripetal and ultimately frustrating. It sets its own terms and hence tends to reject or underrate any aspects of the experience which happen not to meet those terms. Paradoxically, not only the repudiation of novelty, but also the embracing of it, are equally traceable to acquiescence in the whimsies of intuition.

The corrective to a naïvely intuitive experience is one in which the faculty of deliberative thought has a part. If intuition, by definition, seems to afford a spontaneous and complete penetration of the experience by a single leap as it were, the intervention of deliberative thought implies a conscious and rational qualification of the experience. For however spontaneous and unrationalized the initial impulses (of composer or perceiver) may be, a musical work in full and final formulation is a pattern of tones whose relations evolve by such close d highly organic deductive reasoning, that a unique phı menon is put into action which must be recognized an llowed as a logic of tone relation – a musical logic – thı its own province is analogous to the other two logics of tl nd, the linguistic and the mathematical.

The terms under which the fully consummated musicı perience must take place are hence conditioned by logiı ogic induced by and reflected from the logic of the con ser's musical processes themselves. The perceiver on h n part now exercises the faculty of deductive reasoning ı inseparable part of the experience. Nor has the intuitiv gredient been eliminated. It has instead been subjected t ucation and may presently resume its initiative on a fres ıne. Music education is then, so far, an education of th uition through the impingement of a considered musicı gic upon it.

The most fundamental and explicit study of music is there re the study of the logic of music. The essence of th gic may reach any level of penetration from elementar tening to advanced composition or style criticism, and ma rmeate the educative process in any of the various aspect music study.

The casual reconstruction of musical logic may go on as ore or less spontaneous intuitive-deductive activity at what er level of grasp the perceiver has competency. The pur t of the logic of music as a study, however, implies it ional formulation. The attempt to reduce the logical proc es to principle is in itself an educative induction into thei erations. In recompense for the task of rationalization, th sh perception which such consideration elicits is in turı lected in an intensified intuitive-deductive power, in con uence of which a further increment is added in refinemen the aesthetic experience.

Though the logic of music reveals an essence which remain gularly constant, at least through all Western music, it i vious that no point of stabilization or completion of it nifestations is conceivable. Music education must there fore take account of the different phases of musical logic characteristic of various epochs – not merely of the logics of a Bach or a Beethoven, fundamental, though incomplete in themselves, as they are. These changing manifestations are tokens of an evolution of musical thought which is inseparable from the history of music itself. Since such pursuance of musical logic in the historical frame requires as one of its chief implements the understanding of style, style observation will also become an intrinsic part of the approach.

To the obligation of the different branches of music to devote themselves to the study of musical logic is now added the obligation to do so with the full light of historical and stylistic evidence thrown upon every situation. The study now takes place in an appreciably enlarged context, which conditions with new breadth the nature of the response to music.

It is apparent that the aesthetic experience, sensitized to a wider range of stimulation, is no longer involved only with the music which is at the moment in hand: it carries at the same time unformulated overtones of comparison with other absent music. One is not merely engrossed in the experience of a single composition or musical phenomenon. The entire background is faintly but significantly engaged. As a complement to this sense of comparison a tone of detachment from complete self-identification with the sensuous impact and the logical processes of the music enters the experience – the "psychical distance" of the aestheticians – giving the experience a generality and durability which counterbalance its immediacy and transiency.

In its more sophisticated developments, the experience may also contain some degree of conscious aesthetic formulation and interpretation, without detracting from the spontaneity of the response. An experience of such amplitude will further involve, or be followed by, an element of evaluation. If this critical factor is manifested as an accumulating sense of value in the course of the experience, the latter will itself be enhanced. If appraisal follows the experience proper, a shade of added significance will be transmitted to later musical experiences.

The exploration and application of the logic of music in a constantly expanded and enriched context thus raises the aesthetic experience to a point of high sensitiveness and maturity. Only a prolongation of the conditioning of the experience in these same terms can further deepen it.

The greatly prized concomitant of the mature aesthetic experience is taste. It develops beside and within the deepening experience. Cultivation of the experience is at one and the same time the cultivation of taste. In the development of taste, its intimate motivation comes from the educated intuition, while its broad base is formed by the sense of relative values contributed by context. The ultimate clarification, fortification, and justification of taste arise hence from the exercise, at a high level, of the critical faculty. Musical taste in full maturity might then be considered as the reflection of an intuitively sensitive aesthetic experience, of rich context and strong critical content.

Implicit in the foregoing concept of music education is the assumption that the central substance of the education is music itself – the accumulated body of works spoken of as "music literature." It is accordingly evident that the process of education, set forth above in abstraction, does not take place as an abstraction. It is rather a several-sided activity in which various applications are given to a core of ideas. Music education, as it explores musical logic in context, will spread therefore into concrete activities, enmeshed with one another and with the living substance of music. These activities – listening to and performing music, writing music, and writing critically about it – will thus be seen to be the objective field of operation of the experience and hence of the process of education.

According to the preceding course of thought, music education at the full may now be conceived as the consummation of a salient aesthetic experience, based on the interaction of an educated intuition and a rationalized musical logic, saturated with a varied and rich context, and subjected to critical clarification. Such a matured experience is the end-in-view of the higher liberal music education.[1, 2]

The whole educational process, and by inference the philosophy behind it, may finally be gathered together in the outline of Scheme I on the opposite page.

II. *A Critique of the Curriculum*

The edifice of music education in the colleges was originally constructed chiefly under the influence of patterns derived by attenuation from professional music education, and hence in essence not native to the liberal arts situation. The nucleus of such education was for some time the "theory" of music and a study suggestive of music history. In the course of events the pillar of history has been shored up, patches, such as music "appreciation" and some more or less fragmentary studies in the literature, have been applied to the main structure, and a wing – usually painted a brighter color – the size of which may dwarf the original plan, has more recently been attached to accommodate "applied music" (a branch conservatively excluded in the earlier curricula, though an essential factor in professional education). In spite of some pleasing interior furnishings and amiable tenants, the structure as it now stands is, by and large, an anachronism in the environment of the liberal arts college.

The study of music, which deserves as much compactness, unity, and focus as any branch of the liberal arts, has been allowed to suffer fragmentation, diffusion, and overspecialization. Its parts remain more or less arbitrary units, wastefully

---

[1] Cf. the author's "Mutual Objectives of Music Education in School and College: A Critical Appraisal." *Volume of Proceedings*, Music Teachers' National Association, vol. 33, 1938, p. 175ff.

[2] Cf. the author's "The Study of Style as the Clue to Higher Music Education." *Ibid.*, vol. 38, 1944, p. 200ff.

[SCHEME I]

Education of the INTUITION through:

A. Rationalization of the processes of musical LOGIC throughout all aspects of music study

B. Formulation of the CONTEXT of music through the contributions of:

- *a. History* and *Sociology of Music*
- *b. Style observation*[1]
- *c. Aesthetics*[2]
- *d. Criticism*

C. Confirmation of the LOGIC and CONTEXT of music through various APPLICATIONS:

- *a. Listening*
- *b. Performance*[3]
- *c. Writing*[4] (in part a discipline) → *Composing* (a creative activity)
- *d. Critical writing*

→ In the interests of enhancing the AESTHETIC EXPERIENCE and cultivating the TASTE

} MUSIC LITERATURE

CREATION, by the composer, of the works of musical art

---

[1] Excludes conventional theoretic " analysis " as an arbitrary methodology of limited historical and aesthetic confirmation.

[2] Includes " theory " as theorization.

[3] I.e., " applied music."

[4] Excludes the writing by " rule " and the categorical explanations of conventional " theory " as anti-aesthetic pedagogical expedients.

overlapping one another, sometimes functioning at cross purposes, and related inadequately.

This is partly due to the fact that many of those who conduct music education in the colleges are likely to be somewhat narrow specialists, lacking in grasp of and sympathy with the subject as a whole. It is the work of the pedagogue-musician-specialist alone which has dispersed the substance of music into weakly related and expediently devised compartments. While it may be conceded that the interrelating of the materials of music calls for genuine knowledge and some authority in the whole subject on the part of the teacher, this is not too exacting a demand for higher education to make. We have accepted long enough in the undergraduate college the overspecialized and undereducated teacher of music.

It is not in the nature of the liberal education to consider the parts of the subject as more important than the whole. The penalty for unsupported treatment of the parts is the need to put together later, at a disadvantage, what earlier has been arbitrarily kept apart. The tidy packages into which the materials of music have been wrapped in the name of practical pedagogy constitute a prime cause of the biased interests and near horizons which beset the student emerging from much current music education.

Though no one college curriculum will contain them all, and no one student can pursue them all, the subdivisions of the subject ramify in what is less a matter of richness than of diffuseness. The fact that these branches are conventionally consolidated into three main categories adds to the dissociation of the materials rather than otherwise. Areas of the subject are officially staked off and the traffic in ideas among them is sluggish. The groups and sub-groups thus commonly recognized may be set down in the arrangement of Scheme II on the following page.

The music educator will readily recognize these branches and identify their pedagogical content and purpose. The general educator, however, cannot be blamed for showing some perplexity in threading his way among them. For his benefit

A. The area of THEORY:

1. "Musicianship"
   a. Elements, b. Ear training, Solfège, c. Keyboard theory
2. Writing and composition
   a. Harmony, b. Counterpoint (modal, tonal); *c. Composition,* [*d. Orchestration* (less frequently found in the undergraduate college)]
3. Analysis
   a. Harmonic analysis, b. Form analysis

B. The area of HISTORY:

1. History as such
   a. History, b. Subdivisions of History studied as "*Literature*"
2. Ancillaries to History
   a. "Appreciation"; [*b. Aesthetics, c. Criticism* (these two less frequently found in the under-graduate college); *d. Musicology* (uncommon in the undergraduate college)]

C. The area of "APPLIED MUSIC":

1. Individual study
   a. Solo: various media
2. Group study
   a. Ensemble: vocal, instrumental (chamber music); *b. Choral; c. Orchestral;* [*d. Band* (less frequently found in the college); *e. Opera "Workshop"* (uncommon in the college)]

an indication of the conventional character of some of these fractions of the subject will be included along with the critical observations which follow.

The term music "theory" found its way into American educational parlance as a means of distinguishing the writing and analyzing of music as an academic discipline from the "practice" of music. The significance is very largely a pedagogical one. One must not assume that theory in this sense involves much genuine theorization about the nature of music. That would entail, as part of its apparatus, the enlistment of historical, stylistic, and aesthetic thinking, relatively little of which enters into the conventional concept of theory as a study. In spite of an increasing uneasiness over the arbitrariness and limitation of many of the conceptions on which theory is based, and of admirable attempts to bring them into better line with the art of music itself, theory remains more a system of pedagogical convenience than a formulation and varied application of the fundamental principles of musical art. This is partly due to the prevalent limitation of the evidence to a few selected situations — the classic formulae, the Bachian and sometimes the Palestrinian procedures — instead of a mature search for widely valid principles, durable because they rest upon generalization and lend themselves therefore to versatile and continuous application, no matter what situations may arise in the course of studying the art.

At the elementary end of the scale of theoretical branches there appears a group of activities sometimes collected under the pretentious title of "musicianship." These are evidently contributions to the rudiments of the craft. They may receive enough emphasis to be treated separately, or they may be incorporated with other theoretical study. Actually such pursuits belong before higher education and, as far as practicable, should be finished before one pretends to undertake the serious study of music in the college; or, if the severity of it could be accepted, any necessary study of them in the college should rate as subfreshman work outside recognition by credit.

The writing of music, which is a predominant part of many theory courses, may range from a docile following of rules, to a certain amount of nominally creative work. Its primary purpose is to provide the student with the opportunity of learning about music through constructing it. This is good education and deserves a far sounder and broader base than most programs of theory reveal.

The converse branch of theory, namely analysis, generally suffers from the same malnutrition of basic ideas as that which besets its companion branch. The range of ideas needs if anything to be greater in analysis than in writing. One might go so far as to say that there can legitimately be no such thing as the conventional theoretic analysis, impoverished and distorted as it is by the absence of criteria from history and aesthetics and by the lack of critical technique. When these are brought to bear on the observation and interpretation of the phenomena of music, the result is style criticism – something widely removed from the usual conception of theoretic analysis.

The familiar separation of analysis into harmonic and form analysis further betrays the artificiality of the prevailing analytic approach. Even assuming that the student will try to draw upon whatever wider background he may have, it is a pretense to suppose that the art of harmony can be examined intelligibly without simultaneous consideration of various stylistic evidences, placed against their historical background and given aesthetic interpretation. It is an even greater act of violence to divorce " form " from the widest possible context – form which is not a separate entity at all, but the intrinsic, pervasive pattern of the artistic expression itself. Form analysis still further degenerates when it is chiefly concerned with certain static formulae of design rather than with the nature of design itself.

Theory deserves to take its name seriously and to identify itself with the larger field of theorization which underlies all attempts of higher education to find and apply in practice rational explanations of the art. If theory could be said to have one especial obligation it would be to address itself to the foundational study of the logic of music in the widest supporting context.

At the advanced end of the list of theoretical branches stands composition. Genuine creative writing is for the few and except for modest beginnings falls outside the normal province of the college curriculum. Its justification in higher education suggests that it shall be a fulfillment not only of the intuitive creative gift, but also of that kind of considered creative thought which has been stimulated by the liberal arts context.

Music history has managed, in some degree at least, to reach a more significant point of assimilation among the humanities than has conventional music theory. This is in part because it resembles other college studies, in particular history itself. As it has approached identity with such subjects, however, it has at the same time sometimes tended to lose its identity with music. When this has happened it has been because the study has lapsed into a history about music rather than a history of music. Music history as a chronicle, a set of collected data relating to music, obviously falls short of the meaning of history in higher education.

The study of history must devote itself to a comprehensive interpretation of the works of music literature in the circumstances, artistic, cultural, and social, which brought them into being. It must color its observations with all pertinent aesthetic evidences. The observation of the music itself must be exact and at the same time imaginative – emphases in which the study of history is not always strong. The mature study of music history must also incorporate the description and criticism of style as the essence of its practice; for the stylistic approach is more comprehensive and penetrates more fully into the nature and problems of the materials of history than any other.

The specific study of music aesthetics, as an affiliate of general aesthetics, has been given too slight a place in dealing in an advanced way with the phenomena of music. It has practical as well as abstract contributions to make. In the same degree, both the theory and the practice of criticism have been generally neglected as subject matter for separate consideration. Introduced as advanced phases of music study in their own right, or incorporated in other music studies, these branches, more than any others except history, promise to carry the study of musical works and the ideas involved with them across the parochial boundaries of music into the wider field of the liberal arts. They are invaluable supports of the study of history.

In a certain final fulfillment of the rôle of history in music education it would be appropriate to give attention to a history of the ideas which pervade the realm of musical thought. Such a conclusion would serve to bring to music education the philosophical ingredient which appropriately consummates all of the humanistic studies.

The discipline which assimilates, matures, and fuses the various elements associated with music history, and which embraces theory as well, is musicology. On account of the advanced level at which it carries out these functions, it is for the most part an inappropriate study for the undergraduate curriculum, in which in any case there is scarcely room for it. Musicology, however, furnishes such essential data about music and inculcates a viewpoint of such significance for the liberal arts approach, that the teachers of history and its affiliated branches, and the teachers of writing and even of performance in lesser degree, can hardly afford to be unfamiliar with many of its main findings.

The founding of the earlier college curricula in music upon theory (a specialized and technical approach), and upon factual history (an unvital approach to most students), tended to leave out of account the interests of the intelligent amateur. Theory and history do not seem to begin at the bottom for them. If for no better reason than that there were more of this than of any other kind of student, a type of course whose motto was "appreciation" was presently devised. Courses with this same purpose still persist in one form or another. They usually offer the fundamentals of music in moderated form, coupled with guided listening and a repertory of good music, sometimes introduced in a historical frame.

Courses of this sort have been subject to adverse criticism and even to contempt, for their superficiality – often with justice. There is, nevertheless, an essential task to be accomplished.[1] If some of these courses fall below the level of higher

---

[1] Cf. the author's "The Musical Prerogatives of the General College Student." *Yearbook*, Music Educators' National Conference, 29th year, 1936, p. 120ff.

education, the remedy is an obvious one: an infusion of the study with the fundamental concepts of the art, expressed for this purpose in rather general terms, a motivation of the study of the literature by a specifically historical viewpoint, a deepening of the observation by aesthetic reflections, and the application of an elementary style-critical procedure. Though the study is made more demanding for the amateur in the degree that such intensifications are introduced, this treatment is nevertheless entirely feasible with attentive students, and when skilfully carried out is deeply rewarding. Such a course is firmly attached by its very roots to the body of humanistic studies. It imparts security and meaning to the amateur's musical experience and may serve as a searching orientation in music even for the student of more substantial musical inclinations.[1]

The place of music history among the liberal arts, in all its associated emphases, is evidently a natural one. Its shortcomings as an undergraduate study are likely to lie in its omissions and its limitations of horizon and depth, not in any inherent incompatibility.[2]

The study of "applied music" has been gradually introduced into the liberal arts curriculum in a substantial number of colleges and under various terms. These differ as much as the colleges and their educational philosophies. In its mode of conduct applied music has often revealed little to distinguish it from the study of performance in the music school. There was scarcely any place other than such schools from which to recruit teachers, who understandably enough tended to bring with them and to maintain the attitudes and practices of professional education. The circumstances within the col-

---

[1] Cf. the author's "The Basic Course in a Humanistic Study of Music." *Volume of Proceedings*, Music Teachers' National Association, vol. 42, 1948, p. 45ff.

[2] Cf. the author's "The Study of the History of Music in the Liberal Arts College." Address issued in mimeographed form by the Society for Music in the Liberal Arts College, 1950. Published by Vassar College, 1953.

lege required, to be sure, a modification of the study of performance, both in the amount of time available and in the achievements secured. One result of this compromise has naturally been a constant pressure, still in evidence, to enlarge the scope of the instruction. Not often enough has there been the insight to realize that whatever place may be assigned to the study of performance, it must be a distinctive and idiomatic one, not a borrowed one.

The problem of performance as a study in the college is involved with certain conflicting factors which are at least partly implicit in the study itself. Thus the pursuit of performance may too easily assume something of the nature of a dedication. In consequence there is likely to be a disproportionate concern for performance and a relative isolation of it as a self-sufficient, self-justifying study of music. In the proportion that this study shuts itself in, stimulating and actually indispensable contacts with other parts of the subject and with other college studies are inevitably minimized.

In reflection of this attitude there will often follow the deceptive lure of audience approval. Since music comes into palpable existence only through performance, this prospect must in any event be accepted. This specious distraction connected with music study is, however, an attitude, and as such may be subject to treatment.

A more serious undermining influence connected with the study of performance lies in the fact that it invites a form of instruction and learning by the coaching process. Nothing more foreign or damaging to the ideals of higher education is imaginable. While coaching appears to bring advances, they are ephemeral, difficult to incorporate organically in the student's power of accomplishment, and may readily deteriorate the long-run achievement. This overprevalent tool of instruction must be discarded by the teacher of performance if his subject is to join with other college studies in developing the independent thought of the student.

The most familiar and often decried aspects of performance as a college study are its demand for a special craftsmanship and the inordinate amount of time required in realizing this demand. This is a condition which can scarcely be modified in any appreciable degree. Practical adaptation to the situation would presumably lie in the preservation of a genuinely creditable quality as far as one goes and a resolve to remain within the bounds imposed by the craftsmanship attainable – with some concessions perhaps to fluency. This is no more confining a limitation than that which various other subjects accept within the curriculum.

The teaching of performance in the college is here to stay, whatever educational doctrine may have to say about it. It is important therefore to determine in what direction the study may best be molded, in order that it may become assimilated and may offer the greatest service to the education as a whole. The goal is clear, though its attainment implies a radical reconception of the study as a college subject. Performance may become a genuine liberal arts study only by substantially identifying itself with the other aspects of college music, merging its interests with theirs, and making its ideals and as many of its practices as possible consonant with theirs. This signifies that the central purpose of performance will become the study of music literature, for the sake of contributing in this particular way to the grasp of musical logic under the favorable circumstances of a well-elaborated context. The act of performance will then exist for an end beyond itself, namely that of more richly enhancing the aesthetic experience at the level of higher education.

These are the sprawling materials which call for reselection, focus, correlation, and structural implantation among the other liberal arts in the college curriculum. In an approach to this undertaking, certain complicating factors warrant recognition.

In the undergraduate college, music is but one of a number of subjects to which the student will give attention. The offerings in music must therefore be regulated to the time available for one subject among others. The penalty for pressing beyond these boundaries is the neglect of other equally essential subjects – essential even to music – and a relative impoverishment and disbalance of the liberal education. It is true that the fundamental educative process may go on through music as the medium, over and beyond its literal confines. It is, in truth, this particular attribute which qualifies music for a place among the liberal arts. However significant this fact may be, music is nevertheless so demanding a subject that duly considered lines must be drawn in order to circumscribe its activities to a share commensurate with the whole education. This is sufficient reason in itself for a selection and interweaving of the materials, which seeks depth in preference to bulk or extent.

A related embarrassment which music suffers, one which springs from its very distinctiveness as an art, is its apparent self-completeness. Music may readily become an ingrowing pursuit rather than one which seeks its natural affiliations among the humanities. The more the study of music in college is tinged with the apparatus of professionally specialized instruction, the farther it recedes from an intimate place among the humanistic studies. Music education in the college still stands in the shadow of the precedents, ideals, and criteria of the music school and conservatory, the substantial transplantation of which to the college scene would gratify many musicians and music educators within and without the colleges. Far from being the gospel of music education for the college, this musically egoistic approach is the way toward exaggerating the potential incompatibilities between music and the liberal arts. It will not do to contend, in justification of such specialized practices, that college music is lacking in the technicality and hence the substantialness of professional music education. For music in the college frame has its own forms of intellectual technicality as foreign to the pursuits of the music school as those of the latter are to the college.

A further problem in the formulation of the liberal arts music curriculum, involving the choice and presentation of materials, is found in the fact that there are somewhat divergent types of undergraduate music student whose interests are to be served. There is the so-called amateur, or general student, who seeks a stimulating but passing contact with the arts through music. This same kind of student may, however, desire an extensive, though in no sense pre-professional, contact with music as an impelling force in his total program of humanistic studies.

There are, on the other hand, the pre-scholar and the pre-professional types of student, who may pursue much the same studies as the serious amateur, though with different emphasis and intent. Many of these students are, by temperament and breadth of view, predisposed to the study of music in the terms of a liberal art. It is the problem of the college music educator to conceive music education in such forms as will quicken and develop these different personalities. The fact that they study together in the same groups may be made a profitable rather than a disturbing condition.

At the same time as it is recognized that the education must suit the student, it must also be considered that the education is obligated to shape the student, within those limits which leave him free for unprejudiced later development.

To assume its appropriate place among the humanities – a place which stands waiting to be filled – music in the college is due to take fresh stock of its problems, to recognize its potentially unique contribution to the liberal education, and to concentrate confidently, even aggressively, upon being a liberal art.

III. *Toward an Ideal Curriculum*

Since music itself is the subject of music education, no concept of a vital curriculum can be entertained without considering, first, the various aspects in which music is to be studied; and second, the educative functions which are to be stimulated and exercised in pursuit of the study. These aspects and functions may be conveniently shown in the two tabulations of Scheme III, which at the same time indicate, by the logical though not necessarily conventional names already employed in Scheme I, the branches of music study which make the most specific contributions to each aspect and function. (The order given is an abstract one, not intended to imply an order of study.)

[SCHEME III]

A. The study of music in the following ASPECTS:

1. Its nature and identity as an art:
   a. Aesthetics, b. Style observation, c. Criticism; [Reference to *History* and *Sociology of Music; Performance*]
2. Its changing career in the evolution of culture:
   a. History and *Sociology of Music; b. Aesthetics, c. Style observation, d. Criticism;* [Reference to *Performance*]
3. Its significance to the individual and to society:
   a. History and *Sociology of Music; b. Aesthetics, c. Criticism;* [Reference to *Performance*]
4. Its creative and re-creative manifestations:
   a. Writing, b. Composition; c. Performance; [Reference to *History; Aesthetics, Style observation; Criticism*]

B. The study of music through the exercise of the following educative FUNCTIONS:

1. The receptive and reconstructive:
   a. Listening in all branches of study
2. The projective, constructive, re-creative:
   a. Performance
3. The projective, constructive, creative:
   a. Writing; b. Composition
4. The investigative, descriptive, deliberative, interpretative:
   a. History and *Sociology of Music; b. Aesthetics, c. Style observation, d. Criticism*
5. The deliberative, interpretative, creative:
   a. Criticism, b. Critical writing

The two foregoing analyses are evidently rearrangements, from different points of view, of the ingredients of Scheme I presented earlier. The former of them looks toward music *qua* music, the latter toward the student (and teacher). The complete inseparability of all these elements is axiomatic. From their cross-fertilization, motivated by the educational ideal here affirmed, courses in rich variety and in any grade of advancement may be conceived, and different successions of courses, pointing to a central educational objective, may be evolved. A course becomes merely part of the larger educational concept, one way of access to the common area, one emphasis within the whole.

Whatever the courses may be called, such a sense of the higher integrity of the subject offers, at the least, the promise of a fruitful renovation of accepted types of course and some reshaping of the familiar curriculum; or it might signalize novel fusions of material in courses of new outlook and in curricula of fresh meaning. Which of these lines of advance one may choose to follow, or whether one may attempt some engaging straddle between them, will depend on practical circumstances, on one's background and experience, on the degree of experimental urge, on the characteristic behavior of the educational imagination, or even on the nature of one's unshakable convictions.

Evidently no consensus among college music educators is really to be expected. In truth, various emphases and orders in the marshaling of the factors of the education are possible, with a single main purpose in view. There is of course no one sacred curriculum as the agency for a perfect higher education in music.

Instead of presuming to set up such a curriculum or to formulate such courses as would contribute to it, the purpose of this essay will be fully served if a number of principles of creative curricular organization and their applications are indicated. These will be seen to grow implicitly out of the theory of liberal music education previously presented.

The cardinal principle of higher education in music is interrelation.[1] The allocation of subject matter to certain areas and courses as an educational convenience need not carry with it their isolation or their deprival of nourishment from the

---

[1] Cf. the author's "Correlation in Higher Music Education." *Volume of Proceedings,* Music Teachers' National Association, vol. 22, 1927, p. 22ff.

subject as a whole. A prevailing consciousness, on the part of both teacher and student, of the whole of which each area or course is a part must be regarded as essential to the validity of these parts. Light from various other aspects of the subject must constantly fall upon the smaller area under immediate consideration. That area is entitled to exist only as a momentarily chosen emphasis within the whole. The relations are there. It devolves upon the teacher, in his conception of the subject and his method of imparting it, to reveal and exploit them.

A second principle, bearing now upon the successive interrelations of the materials, is progressive continuity. It is feasible to conceive courses in consultative cooperation, so that those that will be studied later actively complement their predecessors. This is not merely the familiar device of prerequisites in more or less fixed sequence, arranged from an elementary necessity to provide the required prior information. It is rather the projection of the influence of interrelation forward in a homogeneously expanding organism of ideas and experience.

As a corollary to various manifestations of interrelation and continuity, a quality of cumulation ensues. Though scarcely appreciable at any single moment, its influence becomes increasingly potent in the unfolding of the experience of education. This is not an attribute that is likely to materialize by chance: it is the consequence of careful consideration of course emphasis and the maintenance of a constant view of the whole subject. A deeper unity is thus achieved which might be called an integration of the entire education in music. This ultimate integrity, seen imperfectly in prospect and understood only in retrospect, is a major clue to higher education.

The thoughtful application of these principles, in the spirit of an ideal education, would effect changes, some of them radical, in the orthodox curriculum and in the courses within it.

The first consequence of an acceptance of the principle of interrelation would be a recognition of the importance of providing a general orientation in music at the outset. No presentation of the rudiments of music, offered by the initial course or courses in "theory," comes remotely within sight of the range of ideas, the precision and durability of concept, or the validity of explanation of the nature of music, essential to an effective introduction to the subject. Such courses commonly busy themselves with "theoretical" minutiae and drill, in a shallowly "technical" way, without coming to grips with the significant concepts which lie behind these details.

Nor can the ordinary course in "appreciation" fulfill this obligation. It is too imprecise, too inexacting and diffuse, to provide a secure point of departure. Music, especially at the lower levels of study, is singularly beset by half-truths, temporary truths, incompletely defined concepts, inherited and unchallenged *clichés*, and a theoretical and aesthetic terminology which is the despair of precise thinking about the subject. These disabilities call for constructive attention so that the student may proceed from a secure beginning.

A fresh start is invited in the creation of an orientation course which will serve as the cornerstone of higher education in music. It will offer a fundamental contact with the art, in which all presentations are fully motivated by a body of ideas that will never need contradiction or essential modification, but will expand and mature in later applications. They will be interrelated ideas of wide validity — principles which will obviate the superficial rules of the conventional order. The student will be introduced to the fundamentals of musical logic in as ample a context as possible. Since even good students come with inconsistent and inadequate preparation, the far-reaching orientation course would perform, on the one hand, the negative but useful service of nominally harmonizing the equipment of students, and on the other hand, would forestall misconceptions which, if allowed to stand, would be likely to plague the student in all his later thinking.

The impact of such an initiation into the subject, even as little as a half-year of it, would be felt throughout the student's entire subsequent study. The time given would be fully redeemed in the minimization of omissions, uneconomical overlappings, and conflicts. The good college student in music is able to stand the challenge of such an introductory discipline. Its "technicality" will lie fully as much in the realm of ideas as in that of craft.

After the phase of orientation, the next step in the student's advance will take the form of expansion. The explorations of this phase will be governed even more discriminatingly by interrelation and progressive continuity. In this intermediate ground the range of ideas will enlarge, the emphasis on different aspects of the field will multiply, and the student's grasp of logic and context will strengthen. The studies which fall in this phase should be structurally shaped toward these ends. It makes little difference what particular branches of the subject are involved at any one moment. Furthermore, the number of courses available to the student is less important than their character. The emphases brought out and the ideas associated will signify more than the covering of ground or the imparting of information. Courses supporting this stage of the student's growth face the exacting challenge of both spread and advance, coupled with interrelation.

The final phase of the student's undergraduate education will be dominated by synthesis. This is the educator's as well as the philosopher's ideal. The phase of synthesis plays a part in consummation of the educational experience significantly analogous to that of orientation at the beginning. It issues from the creative application of the principles of interrelation, cumulation, and integration. It brings to maturity the faculty of logic and the appreciation of context. This late phase enjoys a special vantage point from which it is finally possible to see what is to be related; at the same time new and more advanced relations are also perceivable. A reorientation in depth takes place.

This culminating ingredient in the student's experience ought to manifest itself, not only as a permeating influence within the fabric of all his advanced studies, but also in some special final course dedicated to the specific goal of synthesis.

Such a course will offer the same exacting challenge to both teacher and student as that carried by the initial orientation course. Pedagogical wisdom and a great deal of pure scholarly and artistic authority are called for. The conduct of the course should not consist merely in presentations and demonstrations, by the teacher, of the evidences supporting synthesis: it will also be the obligation of the student to carry out some culminating piece of work – a mature investigation, an essay, an examination – the viewpoint and technique of which are motivated by the concept of synthesis.[1] In addition, this and other advanced work may now properly incorporate a limited element of specialization, appropriate as one part of the final phase of the education. Synthesis prevalidates specialization.

In all the student's later studies independence of thought, and the channels for manifesting it, must be developed.

A condensed repetition of these abstractions now follows in reminder:

[SCHEME IV]

A. Motivation of the liberal education by the PRINCIPLES of:

1. Interrelation
2. Progressive continuity
3. Cumulation
4. Integration

B. Concurrent applications of these principles throughout the following successive PHASES of the education:

1. Orientation
2. Expansion
3. Synthesis
4. Specialization

Music education approaching such an ideal is evidently a challenging and demanding undertaking. It calls for wide knowledge and for sympathy with the subject in all its aspects. It is an education which can be realized only by a high order

---

[1] Cf. the author's "The Senior Field Examination in the Liberal Arts College." *Ibid.*, vol. 36, 1941, p. 254ff.

of planning and creative experimentation. It demands a subtle and mature pedagogy not committed to stated methods. This pedagogy will invoke such familiar tokens of higher education as:

[SCHEME V]

1. The collection and description of evidence
2. The critical appraisal of evidence
3. The entertainment of hypotheses
4. The establishment of premises and deduction of conclusions
5. The clarification of concepts, coupled with precision of terminology
6. The subjugation of detail to principle
7. The interpretation of data through higher generalization

These and other similar procedures may permeate all aspects and stages of the instruction, without the slightest impairment of the prerogatives of the art.

It remains to consider how this education may best be adjusted to the individual student's interests and preferences. In spite of the higher unity conceived for such a curriculum, and of the consequent interdependence of its courses, each course may at the same time appear to be a reasonably rounded conception in its own right, so that the student who may not wish to go forward with his studies will be left with an ample sense of achievement upon the completion of one or more stages of music study. A certain amount of elective diversity may hence be accepted from the free-lance student.

But for the student who desires considerable systematic contact with music, a more specific program is desirable, whether the student finally becomes a " major " in music or not. A prescribed core of studies, pursued in a more or less consistent order, with limited alternatives, is called for in support of the developing unity of the education. At this higher level differences of objective may be somewhat minimized, in the interests of laying the foundations which are the special contribution of the liberal education. Larger diversity or marked specialization coming later will be enhanced in unique ways by resting against the background of such previous training. If fairly specific requirements are posed, especially in the early and final stages of the student's program, an education is shaped which for many purposes is complete in itself; or else a secure and distinguished base is laid for various, even any, later musical studies or pursuits. Divergent student temperaments do not at this stage call for great humoring at the expense of an education of depth, breadth, and unity.

A final obligation, implicit in the liberal music education, is that of bringing to music study stimulating influences from the larger field of the humanities. These may take the form of contributory information, background substance, analogous ideas, evidence necessary to complete some broader view of which music is only a part, methodology in parallel situations. The allied subjects will not all contribute equally. Their services will vary greatly in the different aspects of music study and at the different levels of the education. The contributions from related subjects may come in the form of courses elected collaterally, or of lectures by colleagues; or they may consist of ample allusions implanted by the teachers of music in their own courses. Since music has much to offer in exchange, cooperatively taught courses on the borderlines between subjects suggest unexplored educational prospects.

It would be a separate undertaking to point out the contacts among the liberal arts which afford valuable support to music education. But in brief substantiation of the principle of correlation, the subjects which promise particularly significant relations may be enumerated:

[SCHEME VI]

1. Cultural history; in a more limited sense, political history
2. Cultural sociology and anthropology
3. The parallel arts and literatures, particularly comparative literature
4. Acoustics, especially interpreted for its conditional musical implications
5. Aesthetics, psychology; aspects of philosophy
6. Criticism in any field; critical theory

The bearing of these studies upon music needs no elaboration. The field of the liberal music education merges with the larger field of the liberal arts. The general or theoretical connections with these studies will prove as valuable as the more literal ones. The teacher of music may properly ask himself what he knows about such extramusical areas as these and what contributions he might draw from them in his own instruction.

It ought now to be clear what is meant by the liberal music education. It is not so clear how we may have it. It is certainly not obtainable in curricular form save by harmonious or at least tolerantly coöperative thought. Yet, among the protagonists in the arena of music education, the thinkers and the doers stand at odds, the literal-minded and imaginative temperaments clash, the conservatives and progressives in musical taste inhabit different spheres of the artistic universe, the pedagogues and the creators find limited common ground, the scholars and the performers speak different languages, even the theorists and historians fail to identify their mutual interests. In the midst of such divergencies, it should be sobering to recognize that many of these conflicting attitudes are attributable to unwarranted differences, more commonly shortcomings, in the educators' own educations.

In escape from the orthodox curriculum – from its sterility and its anachronism – the only alternatives to an integrated curriculum would still appear to be an individualistic conduct of the separate courses, or recourse to some formula of progressive education, or some plausible hybrid. Many will take one of these in preference to the rigors of an indivisible program. Such choice, whichever it is, may perhaps be condoned. For to some there is an understandable and at the same time mysterious virtue in *laissez faire*, from which all good things ought in some way or other to flow; while to others the pragmatism of progressive education carries within itself the solution of all problems. In the meanwhile, whatever philosophy or lack of one may prevail, higher music education waits to develop some of its most vital potentialities.

IV. *The Autonomy of the Liberal Music Education*

It will only lead to misunderstanding to assume that the liberal education envisaged here is the adaptation – even a partial one – of something else, least of all of a professional education in music. It is no such artifice. To misunderstandings of this sort are attributable, for the most part, the misgivings of professional musicians and doctrinaire educators concerning such an educational outlook. Their benevolent inclination to press irrelevant criteria upon college music is due to obsession with their own concepts of music education and to sheer unawareness.

The bona fide liberal education in music is a derivation, to be sure, but one arising in every thought and aim directly from the deepest foundations in the humanistic disciplines. Its native environment is that kind of undergraduate college which profoundly cherishes the liberal arts, and its human material is in general the kind of student found there.[1] Its opportunity lies with this type of student and the latter's most rewarding access to music is to be discovered in this education.

It is an education wholly functional to its environment. It has its own underived values and a distinction which is its special property. It is an education which reaches forward and promises constantly deepening musical experience. It therefore has meaning in the highest sense of education. It is an education which may be said to lay unique foundations for the later pursuit of music within or without the original frame; for it closes scarcely any doors to future musical activity. In spite of its devotion to the ideal of unity, it nourishes a versatile rather than a standardized product as one of its peculiar accomplishments. It is of the essence of higher education.

There is no better way to reëmphasize the purpose of the liberal music education, and to throw into relief its distinctive quality, than to point out the ideal of accomplishment which

---

[1] Cf. the author's "The College Type of Music Student." *Ibid.*, vol. 29, 1935, p. 127ff.

liberal arts students of music, taken collectively and under favorable conditions, may be said to approach. It is an ideal of power – power which derives from such attributes as those asserted in Scheme VII.

[SCHEME VII]

1. A creditable acquaintance with the most significant music literature, and a catholic taste tempered by experienced discrimination
2. An enriched artistic perceptiveness, both intuitive and rational
3. A grounding in the basic musical crafts, with nominal facility in them as tools of approach to the art
4. An acute discipline in general listening, and in more precise listening to the degree that the individual's faculties permit
5. A grounding in scholarly knowledge and discipline, comparable to that attainable in other undergraduate fields, together with sensitivity to the scholarly viewpoint
6. A sharpened critical faculty and an inclination to interpretative thought
7. An insight into some form of constructive or creative thought, as an aesthetic discipline or personal satisfaction
8. An awareness of the *milieu* of ideas which surrounds the art, and facility in interpreting and employing them
9. A philosophical sense of the higher unities of the art and of the community of arts

These endowments, hardly likely to be found evenly balanced in the make-up of any one person, should nevertheless be discernible in valuable proportion in all of the aspects of the higher education in music. They are the symbols of a deepened and durable and personally significant aesthetic experience. They embody the ideal of the liberal music education.

CPSIA information can be obtained
at www.ICGtesting.com
Printed in the USA
BVHW08*1527041018
529297BV00008B/118/P